A

GARDENER'S
ALPHABET

Elizabeth Harbour

MICHAEL JOSEPH
LONDON

MICHAEL JOSEPH LTD

Published by the Penguin Group
27 Wrights Lane, London W8 5TZ, England
Viking Penguin Inc., 40 West 23rd Street, New York,
New York, 10010 USA Penguin Books, Australia Ltd, Ringwood,
Victoria, Australia Penguin Books Canada Ltd, 2801 John Street, Markham,
Ontario, Canada L3R 1B4 Penguin Books (NZ) Ltd, 182–190 Wairau Road,
Auckland 10, New Zealand

Penguin Books Ltd, Registered Offices: Harmondsworth, Middlesex, England

First published 1990
Copyright © Text and illustrations Elizabeth Harbour 1990

Typeset by Cambrian Typesetters, Frimley, Surrey
Made and printed in Singapore by
Kyodo Shing Loong Printing

A CIP catalogue record for this book is available
from the British Library

ISBN 0 7181 3347 1

For my mother and father
and Neville

A
gardener
gives his
garden
love and care
which in return
gives him joy

An early autumn morning and there is a rustle of green leaves as the gardener steadily picks the fruit for the apple store. The autumn air is filled with the scent of warm apples and the sound of windfalls dropping to the ground.

A humid day that promises rain;
birds' nests which are hidden
deeply within the trees' branches
are now deserted. This is a perfect
time for tending to the topiary. The
gardener skilfully clips the tree to
retain its shape and encourage new
growth in the right places.

Dappled sunlight filters through the walnut tree. A soft breeze carries the scent of cut grass; hollyhocks and sunflowers race to climb the mellow-bricked garden wall. A lazy summer's day when only the cat remains awake and playful.

A dusky warm summer's evening, when gnats gather in shady spots and little white greenfly stick to the leaves of the beech hedge. A daddy-long-legs panics as the gardener's shears touch the twig upon which he rests; a blackbird sings his final song from a nearby tree.

Blustery days bring colour to the gardener's cheeks; autumn leaves gather on the paths and dance on the lawns in the easterly wind. The creosoted shed smells of long-gone summer; spiders' webs are deserted and everything prepares for sleep.

The maze is clipped into shape to prevent wandering tendrils of new growth concealing hidden paths and lost corners. The puzzle waits for summer when echoes of laughter from happy children will fill the air as they search for the middle.

The rose arbour is filled with roses looking down on their visitors and the sound of bees buzzing to the flowers as they gather pollen. It is a walkway of heavy scent; here roses bloom and die throughout the summer, while small birds nestle carefully between the thorny stems.

H

The walled vegetable garden is lined with loganberries. Here the earth is bare in winter, concealing hidden wonders deep underground. In the spring the sun warms the earth, encouraging the vegetables to come to the surface for the gardener to gather for the house.

Crimson Glory roses climb and fasten around the garden wall, framing the doorway. This reveals another part of the garden, a secret haven where there are towering lupins of different colours. The hard earth of the flowerbeds is broken up by the gardener's hoe, helping young plants to grow and summer showers be absorbed by the soil.

J

The Victorian greenhouse is a warm,
humid place with smells of peat,
growing plants and condensation.
This is where new seedlings are
grown for the garden, safely away
from hungry birds and harsh frosts,
and where large chrysanthemums
thrive and bloom.

The leaves of the flowering cherry
fall with sadness in the cold
autumn wind which hurries grey
clouds across the sky. The garden
prepares itself for approaching
winter and the gardener gathers
leaves for large smoky bonfires.
Heather comes to life giving the
garden its last flood of colour.

The low evening sun settles on the tree tops as dusk approaches; the flowers appear more vivid in colour once the heat of the afternoon has passed. The song of birds in the trees and the sound of the whirring blades of the lawnmower fill the air.

The gardener captures the roses
which have strayed from their
support of the trellis wall, climbing
high to offer their petals to the warm
morning sunshine; fiery yellows,
soft pinks and deep crimsons grow
in abundance, forming a cheerful
patchwork of colour.

Under the shelves in the greenhouse, old terracotta pots lie covered in cobwebs whose guardians scuttle away from the gardener's feet. Yellow tomatoes grow crimson, ready for the kitchen's salads; green ones will be turned into chutney.

The Cox's Orange Pippins are
gathered into a wicker basket, the
apples still holding the faint scent of
spring when the blossom was
pollinated by the bees. The fruit has
been coloured by the sun and their
marbled skins are shiny, firm and
cool to the touch.

P

The gardener is grateful for the shadows cast by the golden-leaved yew tree, while the grass beyond fades in the sunshine. Fuchsias bud and bloom repeatedly through the summer months and the flowers on the frail standards dance like bells in the summer breeze.

The stone bird bath, its edges
covered with wandering algae, is for
the birds who fill the garden with
music. In warm weather they drink
and bathe while drowned flies float
on the surface. The gardener puts
fresh water into the bath each day
during the hot summer months.

On an early spring morning the flowering cherry tree entices some of the garden's visitors, especially the cat who is attracted by the fluffy pink blossom. New spring flowers line the sleepy winter beds as the sunshine warms the dewy grass.

A secret dell is enclosed by large
yew trees and rhododendrons, a
rich green lawn is bordered with
catmint and Queen Elizabeth roses.
Water sprinkles on thirsty plants,
wood pigeons coo to one another in
the trees, and bees dance merrily on
the flowers; a place that never
changes from morning to dusk.

Everything wakes up in the early morning sunshine, cats stretch and stalk the grass for a little field mouse or drowsy bee. The gardener is preparing to rake the earth which has finished its work for the year and is now ready to be planted for the next season.

The weeping willow tree has a sleepy influence; its long green leaves whisper in the wind and form cool shade on a hot summer's after-noon. Its branches bend and touch the ground, often becoming a favourite hiding-place for children.

Long runner beans produce continu-
ously throughout the late summer,
their green shoots curling and
latching on to the bean poles. When
it seems that all have been picked,
red flowers reveal themselves
behind large, damp, heart-shaped
leaves and more will grow.

The apple store is a small house in the garden, with windows covered with cobwebs and shutters to close out the light. Apples and pears are kept in neat rows until they are required up at the house. Long-legged spiders climb unsteadily over a sea of green and red fruit.

Delicate sweet peas climb bean poles like the runner beans, their colours shimmering in the pale light of the summer's evening; they could be easily mistaken for a gathering of fluttering butterflies. The earth smells sweet where the gardener has been watering.

Poplar trees reach high to the sky and sway in the wind. The gardener clips them where they overcrowd the walk. The trees are green and luscious in the spring but are sad stick-like figures in the winter.

Ivy loves all the shady places in the garden, creeping into crevices and smothering innocent plants. A snail crawls a silky path across a spear-like leaf, searching for a safe place, away from thrushes, to rest until dusk.

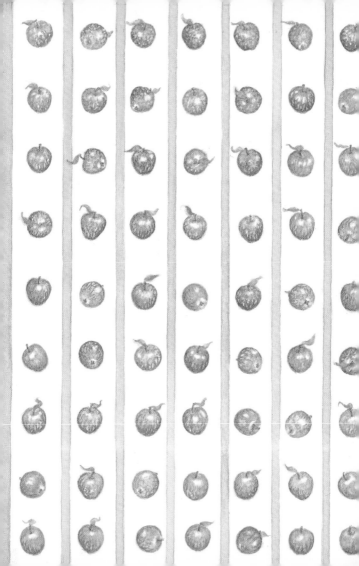